Philosophy for children

From child to children

Once upon a time!

Don't teach what you don't do!

Coloring story!

By: Bernardo Octaviano Pereira

This book belongs to:

____

I dedicate this work, firstly, to my parents who I love so much, to my teachers, to my dear aunts and to all my friends, may God bless you all infinitely!

Bernardo Octaviano Pereira

13/04/2024

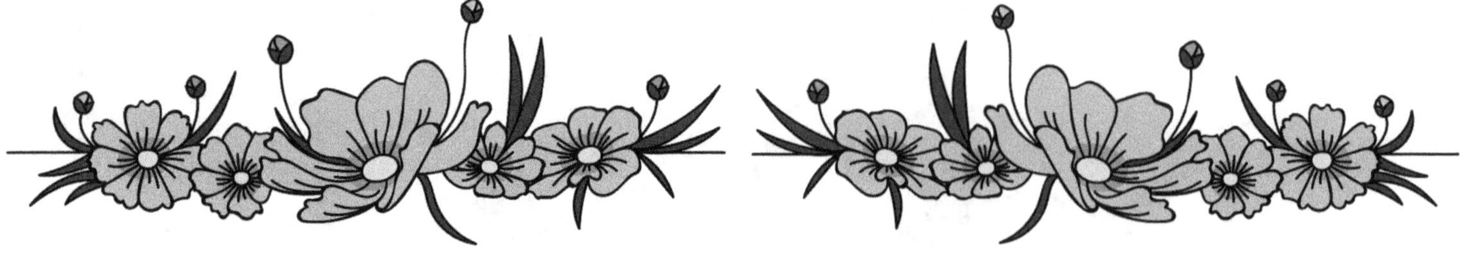

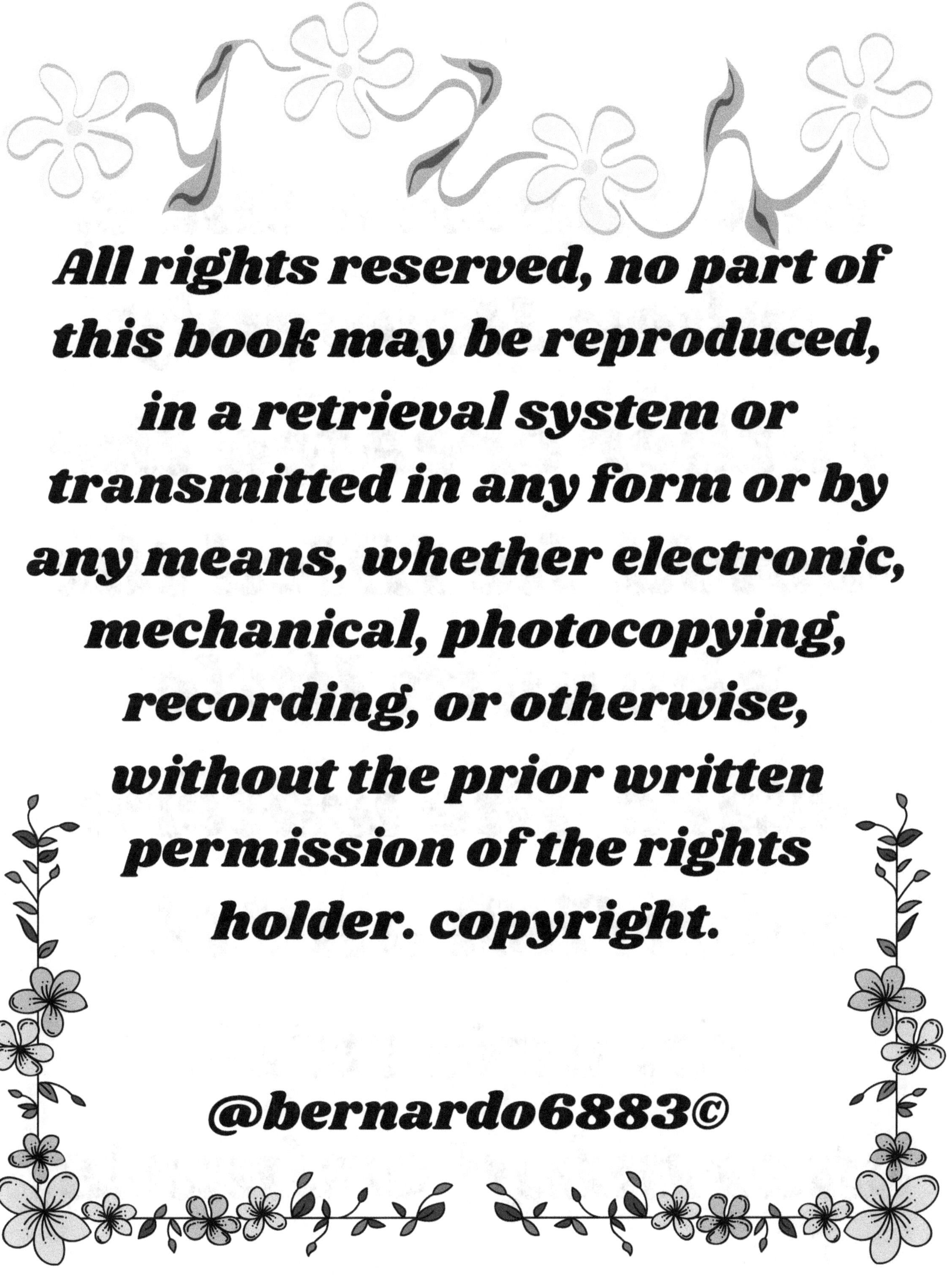

Once upon a time, when Heavenly Father created the world, he filled the sky with little stars, the waters with fish and the forests with charming animals;

One of these little animals was the crab, which had a peculiarity: it walked sideways, unlike all the other little animals that moved forward.

Embarrassed by his uniqueness, the crab decided to teach his little ones to walk forward, like most other little animals did, with patience and affection,

He shared his experiences and taught the steps so that his little children could learn to walk in a conventional way. Forward, like all the other little animals did;

The little crabs,
dedicated and
curious, will
learn their
daddy's
teachings with
enthusiasm, in
a short time,

everyone was
walking forward,
proud of being
different and
having learned
something new,
walking forward
like their daddy
taught;

However, one sunny day, the daddy crab, distracted, started walking sideways again. One of the little crabs,

When he observed his father, he found it interesting and began to imitate him. Soon, all the little crabs were imitating their daddy's steps, walking sideways.

History teaches us a valuable lesson: it is important to be honest and consistent with our teachings. If we promote something, we must also practice it, because people, especially younger peopl

learn more from what we do than what we say. One day they will see that we are not doing what we are teaching, and they will do what we do, and they will no longer believe in us.

Sincerity and authenticity build a solid foundation in relationships, while lying can undermine trust. And Daddy Crab humbly explained that we all make mistakes, even daddies.

Sometimes, even with the best intentions, we can make small mistakes. We must recognize our own mistakes and, instead of hiding or denying them,

Therefore, this fable teaches us to be truthful in our actions and teachings, cultivating a foundation of trust and respect for each other, which is why we should not lie! But learn from our failures.

The end!